BECOME A'
YOUR EX,
THAT DRAINED YOU.

CLOSURE

CASE KENNY

Copyright © 2023 by Case Kenny. All rights reserved.

No portion of this book may be reproduced in any form without written permission from the publisher or author, except as permitted by U.S. copyright law.

This publication is designed to provide accurate and authoritative information in regard to the subject matter covered. It is sold with the understanding that neither the author nor the publisher is engaged in rendering legal, investment, accounting or other professional services. While the publisher and author have used their best efforts in preparing this book, they make no representations or warranties with respect to the accuracy or completeness of the contents of this book and specifically disclaim any implied warranties of merchantability or fitness for a particular purpose. No warranty may be created or extended by sales representatives or written sales materials. The advice and strategies contained herein may not be suitable for your situation. You should consult with a professional when appropriate. Neither the publisher nor the author shall be liable for any loss of profit or any other commercial damages, including but not limited to special, incidental, consequential, personal, or other damages.

Book Cover by Case Kenny. First edition 2023.

WELCOME TO CLOSURE

... a 2-hour interactive journaling experience designed to empower you to create the closure you deserve in your life.

Are you struggling to move on?

Are you still looking for closure from a past relationship?

Are you starting to doubt what you deserve?

Are you feeling frustrated and ready to give up?

You deserve CLOSURE.

> **closure (n):** a state of being totally at peace with your past and energized for your future.

What follows is part education, part journal. Part perspective, part affirmation.

Closure is designed to take approximately 2 hours and should be done in one sitting for the best effect. It features 19 chapters - each provides thought-provoking perspective and affirmations followed by a variety of exercises and questions.

Read each chapter's perspective slowly and consider your reaction to it. Then answer the prompts that follow. Some of the prompts will be easy to complete while others will force you to be more vulnerable with yourself than you've been in a long time. You'll notice similar themes come up in different ways - follow the prompts and answer as intuitively as you can.

I'm excited for you to create what you deserve in your life. You deserve to live with intention, confidence and know that no matter your past... you are lovable.

CLOSURE is part of a series I call DTR: Define the Relationship (for yourself)... because THAT is your power in life.

YOU decide what your past means.

YOU define what your ex taught you.

YOU define your worth.

And most of all... YOU decide what comes next.

How to get the most out of CLOSURE.

The core principle behind this interactive journaling experience is that closure is NOT a team sport.

Closure is NOT something your ex can give you. It's NOT something I can give you. It's NOT something a checklist, a podcast, or an inspirational quote can give you. You CANNOT receive closure... you can only create it for yourself.

But the good news is you know what it means to empower yourself in life. You've done it before! You've created standards for yourself. You've created boundaries, values you live by, dreams you aspire towards, etc. You can empower yourself in every area of life when you practice radical honesty with yourself.

When you're 100% honest with yourself... closure is close behind.

Approach the following chapters with vulnerability and an eager sense of honesty and you'll find what you're looking for.

Recommendations...

- set aside a full 2 hours to complete.

- minimize distractions - turn your phone on 'Do Not Disturb.'

- Write your answers down. Try to write in complete sentences so you can reference it in the future. (e.g. if a question asks you, "What do you deserve in a partner?" - write full sentences: "I deserve ____"). That way, you'll be able to look at your journal entries as a kind of vision board of what you learned and the new affirmations/mantras you're going to live.

- There is something real about writing by hand. The tactile experience of writing makes your thoughts tangible and human - and most of all… long-lasting. Take your time when writing but don't stress about grammar or making it pretty - your focus should be on the process of introspection.

- if you're struggling to answer a question, that's OK - write your best answer and come back to it later.

Let's get started.

CHAPTER ONE

How do you feel right now?

Let's start by setting the record straight.

You have nothing to feel ashamed about. Nothing. No matter the emotion you're feeling right now… there's no shame. You should never feel bad for how you feel in reaction to what happens in your life.

You should never feel shame for loving someone. You should never feel shame for believing in potential, for believing in goodness and compassion, for believing in hope, or for believing in someone's ability to change. Never.

We're all destined to mess up in life. But if your intentions are rooted in self-love and compassion… no feeling you have should be something you're ashamed of. Your emotions make you YOU, and if they guide you to do things – well-intentioned, compassionate things that might make you stand out, ostracize you in some way, or lead to a less than ideal outcome - you still have nothing to be ashamed of.

You have nothing to be ashamed of when you listen to yourself. You have nothing to be ashamed of when you want to see goodness in someone else and unfortunately that comes back to bite you.

You have nothing to be ashamed of when you act on your curiosity and you fail or it's awkward or humiliating. You have nothing to be ashamed of because you acted on what makes you human.

Don't give up on those emotions. Don't give up on the energy that is true to you. It is YOU. It is human. And how can you feel guilty or ashamed for being human?

How can you feel guilty for believing in hope and potential? That is your superpower, so take this moment and rid yourself of any guilt or shame you've been carrying around with you.

Take a deep breath and simply feel how you're feeling…

Which of these emotions are you feeling right now? Circle all that apply.

- lost
- angry
- confused
- betrayed
- disappointed
- worthless
- unlovable
- falling behind
- mad at myself
- mad at someone else
- getting too old for this
- ready to give up
- blaming myself

Be honest... how are you feeling right now?
Let it all out...

How do you want to feel?
Write at least 5 adjectives

CHAPTER TWO

It's ok to have been wrong

You know how you feel. Good. You can't move on unless you take time to be honest with yourself. A lot of people ignore this first step. But not you…

The next step is admitting you were wrong.

WHOA. Self-blame?! What kind of exercise is this?! No, this is not self-blame. The greatest gift you can give yourself is admitting you've made wrong choices.

I'm sure you'd agree you deserve better in your next relationship, right? We all say we deserve better and we all know deep down that we do… BUT how do you actually receive what you say you deserve? You step up and admit you were wrong. That's how you move past what you DON'T deserve. You simply admit you were wrong. You simply admit you made a wrong choice. You're not saying YOU are wrong as a person or that your standards are too high. Not at all. You simply admit you made a wrong choice in the past.

You're not saying you were at fault for trying. You're not saying you were dumb for not seeing the red flags, for trusting someone, for giving time and energy to them, etc.

You're simply saying you made a wrong choice and now you have a chance to get it right by making another choice. Another more compassionate choice.

Being wrong is NOT a bad thing. We give the word WRONG way too much weight in life. We think "wrong" means low value, low worth, etc. Admitting you made a wrong choice means you're now free to go in a different direction without hanging onto any blame.

It's the greatest gift you can give yourself. It's freeing. It's cathartic.

Saying you made a mistake is how you stop a pattern. It's how you stop accepting less. It's how you stop lowering your standards. You look that feeling in the face, you address it head on, you break it down, and you never go back.

It's not, "I am wrong or I am less." It's just a simple: "I was wrong. Now it's time to be right." In doing so, you're setting the expectation that in the future you're not afraid to try again. You're not afraid because you know the power of claiming what you deserve by making new, better choices in the future - choices that truly live up to your standards AND that live up to what you learned from your past.

Take a deep breath and cast aside any self-blame...

What are some things YOU got wrong in your last relationship? Did you not respect your love language? Did you look too much at potential rather than reality? Did you overlook a red flag? Be honest and vulnerable.

CHAPTER THREE

Today is day ONE

Even though you know the relationship is over and nothing can bring it back... how do you cope with that realization? How do you move on?

Let's start with a powerful realization...

You're not falling behind and you didn't waste time. In fact, you should be thankful this happened today instead of two years down the line.

That's not easy at all... but be grateful you're hurting right now. I know that sounds weird. I know you're tempted to feel guilty and that you wasted time... but it's over and it's done... and it's over and it's done TODAY.

Know this:

A broken today turns into a more powerful tomorrow and hurting today means healing tomorrow.

One more time...

A broken today turns into a more powerful tomorrow and hurting today means healing tomorrow.

That's good news because tomorrow is sooner than you realize, and you should be grateful you're in this position today rather than a year or two years from now. So first... ground yourself in this new emotion.

Gratitude. Be grateful that the relationship is over today - whether you ended it, whether they ended it or whether it was mutual.

It's over. And now you're on DAY ONE of moving forward. That starts today. And today is better than a year from now or 6 months from now.

Give yourself the gift of gratitude. Try to be grateful it's over now rather than some point in the distant future. Because you're going to do a lot in a year!

Yes, a breakup sucks. Getting broken up with sucks. Ending a relationship sucks. Both of you ending a relationship mutually sucks. There's no way around it. I wish I could change that for you, but I can't. BUT there is an interesting upside to a breakup. Something is guaranteed to happen: you will change.

You are guaranteed to come out of the breakup as a different person… in the best way possible. Why? Because you have to! It's the blessing of being human. Leveling up is a human response to a breakup.

Yes, you will hurt. Yes, you'll be tempted to say you're never going to love or date again. You'll be tempted to say that all women suck or all men are the worst.

You'll be convinced you're going to eventually settle because time is running out. But then… your humanness will kick in. Sink or swim. You will change. You will level up.

- You will change out of necessity. You will use the breakup to change for the better.

- You will realize that you no longer have to hang out in the wreckage of what happened. You can build a new world - one that is reflective of what you truly deserve.

- You will change because eventually you'll come to realize that to be happy you have to change. It's a human response. To be happy, you have to pull yourself together. You have to move forward.

- You will embrace the magic of time. You'll come to realize the relationship was neither the beginning nor the end of your story.

- You will embrace the fact that you lived plenty of life before that person and you have plenty of life to live after. Your best days are ahead of you.

- You will recognize that as a human, you are wired to thrive. You are wired to adapt and overcome. You will heal.

There are levels to this life. There are levels to who you are. You still have gas in the tank, and you'd be surprised what levels you can rise to. Just when you think you have nothing left and nothing to reach for… you will find yourself growing. Please believe this. You are guaranteed to grow in the sense that you will further create or recreate your own identity. You will solidify what you stand for. You will grow into what you truly deserve. You will ground yourself even further in what and who is right for you.

You will move past the things that right now you think you'll never get over - pictures of you and your ex together, your shared favorite movie, song, a certain smell, etc.

It's not possible to forget entirely, but soon you won't carry that weight with you so much and it won't be so heavy. And then one day, you'll look back and say, "Wow I'm glad it happened when it did. Look at me now. Look at what happened in the past year. It was a rough start but I'm grateful. I grew through this. And I'm grateful that day one started when it did."

Take a deep breath. You have a whole life ahead of you...

What are 5 things you're looking forward to in your future?

1.

2.

3.

4.

5.

CHAPTER FOUR

Look back to look forward

As much as it's normal to believe a relationship ending is about loss… it's also about what you gain.

There's power in a relationship ending. Have you heard the saying, "When you erase the mistakes of your past, you erase the wisdom of your present?"

How true is that?! When you take the mistake away, you're left without the lesson... and the lesson is everything!

Unfortunate truth: you need lessons in life (especially in your dating life). If all you had were wins, if all you heard was yes, if everything worked out for you… as nice as that might sound… you'd be an absolute mess! You'd be totally ungrounded and disconnected.

You need lessons in life! You need mistakes in life! That is how you arrive at the wisdom of your present. You need THAT lesson.

If you erased the mistakes from your past, you wouldn't have the wisdom of the present.

Can you be grateful for the wisdom of your present? Your past pain, frustrations, and rejection give you present wisdom.

Consider what you've learned from your ex.

Take a deep breath and consider the lessons you've learned…

What did your last relationship teach you? Write as many things as you can think of.

CHAPTER FIVE

The people who hurt you…

Let's build on the idea of past pain and present wisdom by realizing that the people who hurt you are also the ones who help you. Tough to believe?

The people who hurt you are the ones who show you what you deserve.

Plain and simple. Your worth, your standards, your sense of self and centeredness are solidified from THOSE experiences.

A "failed" relationship is nothing to be ashamed of. In a weird way, it's something to be celebrated because they gave you something you need and there's really only one way to get it… through that very experience.

The people who hurt you by saying one thing and doing another, the people who ghost you, who betray you, who break promises, who don't change…

What did that pain give you? It 100% showed you what you deserve, didn't it?

You deserve someone who doesn't lie, who is real with their words, and who has true intentions. You deserve someone who supports you and doesn't have ulterior motives. You deserve respect. You deserve communication.

Although the experiences where you DIDN'T receive those things suck, your worth is no longer just theory. It's real. Those painful experiences make your worth real.

It's one thing to run down the usual internet checklist of things you deserve and not really think twice - it's another thing to experience the direct opposite of those things. You learn through that pain. And what's more... there's a powerful lesson in putting yourself in that vulnerable position in the first place.

To be hurt, you dropped your guard. To be hurt, you connected with someone. To be hurt, you let that person in. To be hurt, you tried.

The world is becoming more and more closed off. People are becoming more and more cynical and hesitant to connect on deeper levels. To be hurt by someone means YOU trusted yourself to be vulnerable and open up. YOU were willing to be first to try or first to be vulnerable. And even though that ultimately didn't work out, it's a powerful truth about YOU. It says something about who YOU are.

YOU are willing to connect, to trust and to be hurt. That is powerful!

Think about how you were hurt in your last relationship...

- Maybe they led you on but never had any intention for more.

- Maybe it was the way a long-term relationship ended.

- Maybe it was being ghosted, lied to, rejected, etc.

Now fast forward to today. Consider some of the things you're committed to doing now. Things like:

- Standing up for yourself.

- Speaking up when you have something to say.

- Disagreeing with someone when you know they're wrong.

- Acting on your intuition when you get a bad vibe from someone.

- Calling someone out when they're being disingenuous.

- Telling someone NO.

- Asking for more.

How do you think those practices came about? You do those things, and you'll continue to do them because the people who hurt you reminded you of your worth and now it's real to you.

Real lessons give you real perspective and real perspective gives you real habits that reinforce it.

The quality of your present and future life 100% comes from those real habits. Not theoretical habits. Real habits.

The pain will subside, but the reminder will stay. The habit will stay. Be grateful for it…. in the only way you can. In a practical way. In a way that isn't theory or cliche… in a way that is real to you.

That's you standing up for yourself, saying NO, not getting drawn into toxic relationships, expressing your worth in what you do and say and wear, and practicing your passions and hobbies as loud and vibrantly as you want. That's you living your worth and recognizing the path to get here was painful, but it's worth it because your new standard can never be taken from you.

Take a deep breath and feel the warmth of your self-worth...

What do you deserve? Write 5 "I deserve ____" statements. Thought starters:

- Someone who is real with their words and has true intentions
- Someone who supports me & doesn't have ulterior motives
- Someone who respects me
- Someone who is honest with you from day one

1. I deserve

2. I deserve

3. I deserve

4. I deserve

5. I deserve

What are you committed to doing in your dating life? Write 5 "I'm committed to _____" statements
Thought starters:

- Standing up for myself
- Speaking up when I have something to say
- Acting on your intuition when I spot a red flag
- Calling someone out when they're being disingenuous
- Telling someone NO
- Asking for something I want

1. I'm committed to

2. I'm committed to

3. I'm committed to

4. I'm committed to

5. I'm committed to

CHAPTER SIX

It's ok to have loved and "lost"

It's easy to look back and think the younger version of you was more worthy than who you are today. We beat ourselves up in the present for having blown it in the past and as a result, we think we were more worthy then than we are today.

But here's the thing...

You are ALWAYS deserving and ALWAYS worthy. That never changes.

Who you are today is just as worthy as who you used to be - no matter if you feel old and washed up, no matter if you feel you've tried and failed as many times as humanly possible, no matter how many times you've been absolutely crushed, loved and lost, etc.

Your worth doesn't stay in your past with that failed relationship. Your worth doesn't stay in the past with that younger, cooler version of yourself. Your worth doesn't stay in the past with that version of yourself who could party 'til 4 am and get up and do it all over again.

Your worth follows and grows with you… but now it has the added benefit of being wiser.

It might be cliche to say but it really is a true statement: it's better to have loved and lost than to never have loved at all. Why?

"Lost" is an interesting word... What exactly are you losing when you go through a breakup?

- Do you "lose" when those experiences give you a better understanding of what's right and what's wrong for you?

- Do you "lose" when you realize you deserve someone who doesn't give you mixed signals?

- Do you "lose" when you realize you deserve to be chosen all the time... not just on Saturday night at 2 am?

- Do you "lose" when you're proud of yourself for being vulnerable with someone?

No. How can you say you lost? Through those experiences... you gave yourself the gift of wisdom and certainty. Through those experiences, you're now certain of what you need, of what you bring to the table, and of what impresses you and what doesn't.

Doesn't it feel good to walk around and know who the heck you are and what you deserve? Doesn't it feel good to be certain about yourself?

Yes... heck yes it feels good! Your worth is right here and now it's supercharged. It's supercharged because it has the benefit of past wisdom and present certainty.

- You know WHY you're amazing... not just that you're amazing. You know WHY you have high standards... not just that you should have high standards.

- You know who deserves your time and energy... not just that you're supposed to protect your time and energy.

You know what you represent and who you are. You have wisdom. You have certainty. And most of all... you know that you deserve to love and be loved again. The person you are today is just as deserving as the person you were then. Your worth is amplified by what you lose... not diminished by it.

Take a deep breath. You deserve to love and be loved again.

What are 5 things YOU bring to the table?
1.
2.
3.
4.
5.

Describe 3 new standards you now live by as a result of your breakup by completing the statement, "I will never _____ again."

1. I will never

again...

2. I will never

again...

3. I will never

again.

CHAPTER SEVEN

What's the story you tell yourself?

What do you think of your ex? What do you say about them?

The perspective you have of your ex in your head and the words you use to describe them and your relationship together REALLY matter.

Here's what we do A LOT after we get out of a relationship...

We shame our ex. We shame ourselves. We let resentment come out in mean, critical, and spiteful ways. Plainly said: we sh*t talk.

We see our ex on social media, and we say things like, "Wow they downgraded. I was so much better than their new boyfriend or girlfriend." We stoop low and say they've really let themselves go.

Or we turn that sh*t talk on ourselves: "I was such an idiot for dating that loser. I have terrible taste in partners. I'm completely blind to red flags."

It's strange how normal it is to hate on your ex and to hate on yourself for dating them. But if you want to get to a place where you have closure… the first step is to let go of that hate, that spite, or that grudge. The first step is to no longer talk sh*t about them or yourself! That's something you can do, right?

You have to let go.

It takes time to create closure, and while you work on that… it's up to you what your perception of your ex is. It's up to you what your perception of yourself is. Letting go of that grudge towards your ex is the greatest gift you can give yourself - to no longer have a reason to hate, shame, or criticize.

All talking sh*t about your ex does is prevent a new beginning. And that's exactly what you need to create closure!

BUT if you hold onto a grudge and you let it manifest in your words and thoughts... you're not on chapter one of that new beginning yet. You might think you are… but you're not. You're still hanging onto that old chapter.

Here's a tough pill to swallow. As much as it feels like catharsis to talk sh*t and as much as it feels vindicating to push them down a level… you're only hurting yourself.

Holding onto those negative emotions only serves to hurt you. The story you tell yourself and the words you use REALLY matter! If you're telling the universe you dated a loser, you wasted your time, they're a horrible person and you're an idiot for letting them in… how does that story do anything but punish you?

Seriously. THAT'S the story you're telling the universe? You dated a loser? You're a loser for dating a loser? What is the universe supposed to do with that story? If you're telling the universe about all the BS you've been through, the boundaries that were broken, the ways you were hurt, the reasons you hate your ex, the reasons you were such an idiot... THAT is what you're going to get dished up again and again.

If you're basically talking sh*t about your ex to the universe, you're not going to be led to the things you actually want. You're gonna keeping find more BS! You learned a lot from your ex, right? You learned what you don't want and what's not right for you, right?

What's the flip side of those things? You learned what you do want! You deserve mutual respect, compassion, boundaries, support, commitment, and communication. So, tell the universe about THOSE things!

Let go of that grudge. Let go of that resentment. Stop talking sh*t! It's only holding you back. It only serves to punish you. True closure comes with time... but until then, can you make a decision to find peace with your perception of your ex?

Can you move yourself to be able to look at them on Instagram and just take a deep breath and be at peace? Can you do that? The moment you make peace with yourself and your ex in your head... you will feel lighter.

You will realize that letting go of a grudge is the first step towards taking back your power. It's the first step towards regaining control of your heart so you can point it in a more fulfilling and compassionate direction... and with that comes closure.

Take a deep breath and make peace with yourself and your past...

Talk sh** talk about your ex. Really let it out - this is the last time.

CHAPTER EIGHT

Closure is NOT a team sport

Ok, you've grounded yourself in how you feel, you've looked back in order to look forward… now what remains is actually creating the closure you need (and deserve).

How do you finally close the page on a meaningful chapter in your life? How do you come to peace with what happened or what didn't happen? How do you move past the temptation to text your ex? To have one more conversation? To find reassurance?

Well… we need to flip the script on what closure actually looks like. You don't actually need closure. You don't need it in the way you once thought you did.

Traditional closure looks like an apology from an ex, one more conversation about what happened or what didn't happen, reassurance that comes from mutual understanding, finding a common "why" or tying up loose ends.

THAT is not the closure you need.

You don't need to hear SOMEONE ELSE put a period or exclamation mark on a chapter in YOUR LIFE. You don't need to hear someone else's reasoning, their frustration, their side of the story again (at least not right now). You don't!

Closure comes from what YOU tell yourself - not what they say. Otherwise, you're essentially asking for permission to move on and that's no way to live.

Closure comes from you - not them.

For some reason, we want to hear them say it. We want to turn to somewhere else for that final validation or reassurance that what's done is done.

We tend to think closure is something that is given to us. We think that we receive closure. But that is not true!

You don't RECEIVE closure. You CREATE closure.

Closure doesn't require an apology. It doesn't require playing back the tape. It doesn't require texting, calling, or anything that involves them right now.

Sure - months down the line if you want to reconnect, if you want to talk… I think that can be healthy. But in the near term, you don't receive closure. You create it yourself. On your own. Closure doesn't come from them. It comes from you.

Let's replace the word "closure" with "peace." I don't think true one-and-done closure is practical to find. But peace? You can create your own peace.

You can create peace by embracing the fact that in life, love, and relationships… your journey is going to be filled with unfinished endings, messy conclusions, stories with no final chapter, and things that just never end up making sense.

True closure is about resisting our human urge to want "closure." It's about resisting the urge to overanalyze, break down what happened, get an apology, try to be on the same page, find proof that it's ok, etc.

Instead, create your own peace by recognizing that some stories don't have clean endings. Some parts of life have no answers and no blueprint - at least not right now.

Life is filled with loose ends and if you spend your time, effort, energy, and compassion trying to tie those up, you're going to find yourself even more drained and frustrated. So instead of wanting to "receive closure," create your own peace with what happened by recognizing that you won't always get the answer you're looking for, the goodbye you want, or the apology you deserve. But you can create your own peace.

Closure is about creating the peace you need - not receiving it. It's about creating your own peace by realizing that who you are is NOT attached to that person giving you closure, you agreeing with what they think, their version of the story, or creating an ending where you finally have their permission to move on.

Say: "Sorry, not sorry… but I don't need that!" That's a compassionate, self-loving sorry, not sorry.

At the end of the day, closure is about YOU.

It is something YOU create for YOU. It cannot be given to you. You cannot receive it. It doesn't come to you in the form of an apology or reassurance from someone.

You have to create that reassurance for yourself. You create it in the form of peace - peaceful acceptance of the open endings, the loose ends, and the unanswered questions in your life.

Closure starts with you, and it ends with you.

You don't need to go back and open a door you already closed. You closed that door for a reason or it was closed on you for a reason. Either way... there's peace in that. There's a stripping of your ego in that. There's a vulnerability in that and THAT sets you free to create your own closure.

It's not easy and it's not overnight, but you'll create your own closure so much more quickly and with less frustration when you stop looking for their permission to do so. You'll create it with much more grace and compassion than looking for it to be given to you.

Take a deep breath and give yourself the closure you deserve...

Do you create or receive closure? Write down your answer.

I _____ closure.

What does closure look like to you? What conclusions are you looking to make - unanswered questions, new standards, knowing "why," etc.

CHAPTER NINE

Grace > Grudges

So, how do you actually create your own closure and why is it more redeeming than receiving it from your ex?

To move on and create your own closure… you have to forgive yourself.

In Chapter one, we talked about not feeling any shame whatsoever about how you feel right now. Let's make that real…

You deserve to be free of fighting yourself. You deserve more than feeling like you're not good enough… for yourself - the one person in the entire world you undeniably are good enough for!

You are so incredibly capable of doing this… of choosing self-grace over self-grudges.

You've learned to do this for others in life, haven't you? You've forgiven exes who hurt you. You've forgiven friends who let you down. You've forgiven people who disappointed you.

You've probably realized that it's soooo much easier to forgive someone else than it is to forgive yourself.

But why is that?

Why do we reserve so much compassion for others and yet we leave ourselves hanging out to dry?

Do you agree that you deserve to feel your best effort is good enough? You do, right? No matter the outcome? You deserve to live without the need to prove your worth, right?

You would never tolerate someone who didn't allow you to live those truths, right? No! You'd leave! You'd cut 'em loose!

And well... since you can't dip on yourself, what's the solution to the things you hold against yourself? It's grace. You forgive yourself. That's the only answer.

Grace over grudges.

That means letting go of grudges aka resentment towards yourself.

- That's a grudge that says your worth is minimized because of something that happened or didn't happen, mistakes you've made, for falling short when you shouldn't have, etc.

- That's a grudge that says you're not who you should be right now.

- That's a grudge that says you're out of time, you've blown it, you're alone in the world, etc.

You wouldn't tolerate someone who held those kinds of beliefs over your head, would you?

So why do you tolerate them from yourself?

It's not easy, BUT forgiving yourself is the only way to move forward. It's the first step towards creating the closure you deserve. It's the first step towards creating the inner peace you deserve.

When you choose grace over grudges, you remember that you can't go back and change the past. BUT you can move forward... and you're not starting from scratch. You're starting from experience.

All the self-blame in the world isn't going to change the past. But grace can change the future. Grace means you move forward... starting from experience. That's POWERFUL!

Ask yourself: what can I forgive myself for?

I'm sure there is something OR many things. What is something you continue to beat yourself up for? What is something you blame yourself for? What is something that makes you doubt your self-worth?

Replace that with grace. Just try. Why not? You've been holding it for long enough. Why not try forgiving yourself for once?

Take a deep breath and forgive yourself...

What are 3 things you can forgive yourself for?

1.

2.

3.

CHAPTER TEN

Would you rather?

It's time to move on. Officially.

You've been on the receiving end of a frustrating dating experience - maybe you were broken up with, ghosted, ignored, given mixed signals, etc.

If you're like most, you overthink the "what ifs." You start assuming and playing scenarios of "what if." You might even be tempted to think you're unlovable or that your standards are too high.

BUT you have what it takes to look that frustrating experience in the face, know you deserve better, say, "Toodalooo," and move on with your life - no overthinking, no self-blame, no lowering your standards. Nada.

The best way to do this is to only give yourself TWO options. Here's how I do it - by playing a mental game of "would you rather?"

First scenario...

Would you rather continue to date someone who is just stringing you along, who isn't serious about you, and will ditch you as soon as they find someone else… OR be hurt today but know you're free to move on to someone who wouldn't want to keep their options open?

Which do you choose? Continue a relationship knowing it's not right for you… OR embrace the breakup? I'm hoping you say option 2.

Another scenario….

Would you rather be with someone who barely meets your standards, who is a nice person by all measures but you're very aware you're settling… OR make the painful decision to be alone for a while longer, to be back to being the single friend again… but in doing so you maintain your standards? I hope you say option 2.

Sometimes the best thing for you is someone overlooking you, deprioritizing you, rejecting you, or breaking up with you. It hurts, but doing a quick "would you rather" in that circumstance can be quite eye-opening.

Would you rather settle for good enough? Would you rather have someone just to have someone? Would you rather be strung along by someone who isn't serious about you? Would you rather accept a bare minimum? Would you rather accept 10% effort? OR would you rather take a short-term pain - a breakup, rejection, being ghosted, being alone again - in order to get the 100% you deserve?

That's the question!

If someone breaks up with you, blindsides you, ghosts you, etc… ask yourself: would I rather continue dating this person only to have them do this to me eventually OR… endure the temporary pain and move on to someone who would never do that to me?

Option 2. All day.

With this practice, you can stop living in the pain of the past and instead focus on the hope and standards of your present and near future.

That is where hope lives. That is where your worth lives. It doesn't live in the past with someone who didn't recognize it or couldn't deliver. It lives in a world where you give yourself two options.

Option 1… you accept good enough, you keep the status quo of your relationship knowing what you know now - they aren't serious, aren't committed, are full of excuses, etc.

Option 2… you take the "L" and you move on towards the "W" you deserve in the future.

Option two reminds you that bare minimum is NOT enough. Having someone just to have someone is NOT good enough. 10% is NOT good enough. 50% is NOT enough. 90% is NOT good enough.
You deserve 100% and option 2 is where what you deserve exists…

I don't know about you, but I'll take a temporary setback any day of the week if it means I have the opportunity to move in the direction of the 100% I deserve. What about you?

Take a deep breath and remind yourself that bare minimum is not enough…

Would you rather... (circle one)

continue to date someone who is just stringing you along, who isn't serious about you, and will ditch you as soon as they find someone else...

OR

be single and happy while patiently looking for someone who understands and appreciates you...

Would you rather... (circle one)

be with someone who barely meets your standards, who is a nice person by all measures but you're very aware you're settling...

OR

make the difficult decision to be alone for a while longer, to be back to being the single friend again… but in doing so you maintain your standards?

Would you rather... (circle one)

have someone just to have someone...

OR

be alone but know you have redeeming days ahead of you?

CHAPTER ELEVEN

There are no coincidences

Let's talk more about what it means to finally find your 100%. Let's talk about how you make your way there - because let's be real... it's not going to be a straight line.

Here's how I think about life...

When you're thrown a curveball in life, something completely out of left field happens or the opposite of what you want happens… you can either chalk it up as a failure, a flop, a conclusion that you're not worthy OR you can simply say… there are no coincidences in life.

You can say: "THIS has to mean something. THIS has to be the right way. THIS has to be a new path, a better path, or a different path that leads to something better."

What a powerful way to look at life! There are no coincidences so whatever new path you're put on - even if it's a path you didn't intend to go down - it's leading you somewhere better.

Reacting to life with a "there are no coincidences" mentality offers you peace and calm. And THAT is what you deserve.

When new things happen - good, bad, or unexpected - they are leading you somewhere. And if you believe that somewhere is good for you.... how can anything be a coincidence? Everything is connected.

Is it a coincidence your relationship ended but then you found yourself and your standards in the process?

Is it a coincidence your relationship ended but then you ended up finding your soulmate?

A curveball in your past or present is inevitably leading you to something more redeeming in the future. Nothing is a coincidence. Nothing is disconnected. Nothing is completely random.

The challenge with this mindset, of course, is that we don't recognize the last part until later - finding your standards, finding yourself, your confidence, your soulmate, etc.

In the moment, it's just a relationship that ended...

BUT can you push yourself to believe that experience will inevitably lead you to something better? Can you push yourself to believe it inevitably will lead you to the 100% you deserve?

When you believe that... how can anything be a coincidence? How can anything be random? How can anything not come to serve you in some way?

There are no coincidences.

This thinking only works if you believe you deserve good things in life. It only works if you believe that life is happening for you, not to you.

So... what do you CHOOSE to believe?

Do you believe that everything is random, nothing is connected, and you're just lost? OR do you believe that whatever happens happens... BUT there are no coincidences, so it's 100% leading you somewhere redeeming?

It's not easy to always choose the latter... but let me ask you this: Which feels better? When you believe that life is random and it's just happening to you, not for you… how does that make you feel? Anxious? Pessimistic? Frustrated?

Or...

When you believe that there are no coincidences because you're always being guided to something better... how does that make you feel? Hopeful? Optimistic? At peace?

Choose what feels good! Choose peace and hope. I'm sure you want to feel at peace and hopeful.

Make this a mantra of yours. There are no coincidences. The more you do, the more you'll start to look back to connect the dots and realize that nothing in life leads nowhere. There is always a more redeeming path in the future.

There isn't any breakup that doesn't lead you to something or someone better or at minimum, there isn't any breakup that doesn't make your standards higher or your self-love more intact.

I hope you choose to say there are no coincidences in your life.

Take a deep breath and embrace the "coincidences" in your life…

What are at least 3 things you deserve in the future that you didn't get previously?

1.

2.

3.

CHAPTER TWELVE

It's time to move on

Let's get serious. How do you move on from something that was once perfect... but then by some turn of events became anything but that? How do you move on when everything inside you wants to hold onto the memories, the sense of worthiness and compatibility you once had? How do you move on when you're still clinging to the past?

We struggle to move on because of our memories. Our memories like to guilt us when we try to move on. They like to be like, "Remember that moment when you first met? It was magical. Remember how funny were they? Remember how you were so happy to have found someone who finally understood you?"

Those memories can serve one of two purposes: they can hold you back OR they can remind you of what you deserve and propel you forward.

If you replay them without framing, you'll start to assume you'll never find THAT again, you'll never find someone who understands you like THAT, and you'll never create moments like THAT again.

If you're not careful, you'll assume that person was the ONLY person who's ever going to be capable of making you happy.

BUT here's what we need to realize...

Your potential for compatibility doesn't decrease over time. It doesn't run out as you get older. It doesn't decrease as a result of a breakup.

It's OK to look back and appreciate what you had with someone... but it doesn't mean you can't find it with someone else - in a longer lasting and more compassionate way. As much as that person was great and had a lot of amazing qualities to them... you can find it again. You can beat yourself up and say, "I miss that person because they actually understood me, they were so interesting, they had such a clever sense of humor, they were so creative..."

And you can turn to all the memories you have to support that. BUT the reality of life is that moving on requires you to affirm you can find those qualities again

... and not a copy-and-paste version but a more redeeming version - a version that is 100% compatible with you and what you need. A forever version.

Free yourself from guilt. Free yourself from assuming you blew it or that you'll never find those things again. Appreciate the memories you have but don't let them hold you back. That is the framing you need to move on.

Think about what a breakup means...

Does something ending mean you aren't worthy of ever having it? OR does something ending simply mean you were not quite compatible?

We need to get real! We need to splash some water on our face, stand up, feel the wind in our hair, and affirm that a breakup is NOT a reflection of worth or what you lack... it's a reflection of incompatibility. That's it.

A breakup has little to do with what YOU deserve, YOUR worth, and what YOU bring to the table… and everything to do with incompatibility.

You simply were not as compatible with them as you wanted to be. You are just as deserving today as you were then AND you can find those things that made that person great... again.

You can find them in a more redeeming, longer-lasting, and more compassionate package. You can find that missing piece of compatibility.

A breakup isn't about you lacking worth; it's about incompatibility.

Despite how close you were to finding that perfect compatibility and how many memories you have that remind you of that fact… you can find it again in a better, more perfect package - a package that is unforced and meant to be. THAT is what you deserve.

Take a deep breath and open your eyes to your past incompatibility…

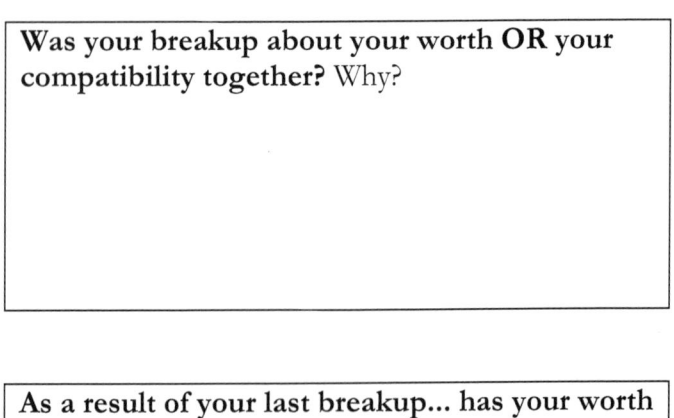

Was your breakup about your worth OR your compatibility together? Why?

As a result of your last breakup... has your worth increased or decreased? Why?

What was at least one incompatible aspect of your last relationship? Focus on your compatibility together rather than aspects of who they were.

CHAPTER THIRTEEN

Good things happen more than once

Let's talk more about those memories. Why do we struggle to let go? As we just talked about, we hold onto memories, people, and experiences because at some point, they were really good for us.

At some point, they were the best thing that ever happened to you. At some point, you thought you had found your person. At some point, you thought you had found what you were looking for and it was amazing. It was what you deserved.

But then life threw you a curveball. It ended. But let's get real... the underlying reason we struggle to let go of the weight we carry with us is because we don't believe that great things can happen to us again.

We don't believe great things can happen to us twice. It's this hesitation to believe that great, rewarding, and compassionate things can happen twice in life that leads us to hold onto those emotions for far too long.

We've duped ourselves into believing that for some reason, we're unworthy of a second shot. We think we're unworthy of finding that person or that feeling a second time. We think we'll never be able to find someone who makes us feel that way again.

I can't think of a more limiting belief in life than that! We need to rid ourselves of this inclination to think that great things don't happen twice.

They absolutely can happen twice... or three times... or ten - as long as you believe you're worthy of them.

That amazing way you felt when you thought you met your soulmate but then it ended in drama? You can absolutely feel that way again.

That sense of calm you felt when you finally found your confidence and your groove before it turned downward? You can absolutely feel that way again.

You CAN free yourself from carrying around shame that you let your soulmate go. You CAN free yourself from guilt that you're no longer the confident person you once were.

Good things happen more than once.

Say it. Make it a mantra of yours.

Good things happen more than once.

We need to let go of feeling unworthy that they'll happen again. We need to let go of fear that we blew it once and for all.

Say it with me...

I deserve to experience the good things I thought I'd never experience again. It might be in a different form. It might look different than what you imagined. It might be a feeling you didn't quite expect... BUT those good things you thought you had and then lost for good?

You deserve to feel them again… and you can, but it starts with letting go.

Take a deep breath and let go…

> **What are some of the feelings and experiences you want to have again… but what about them will be different this time?**

CHAPTER FOURTEEN

It's normal to miss them

You're free to move on!

It's OK to miss aspects of what you had with someone... and still move on. It's OK to miss things, emotions, feelings, habits you once had... and still move on.

You can move on at the same time you still miss aspects of a relationship by realizing this...

Ask yourself: Do I miss the person or the things? Do I miss the person or the habit? Do I miss the person or the attraction? Do I miss the person or the companionship?

Depending on where you are in your healing process, you might say one or the other or both... but eventually you'll realize the following:

You miss the "things" more than the person.
... and you're always going to miss those things in some sense.

But if you assume that closure and being "ready to move on" means you should miss nothing - not the person, not the habits, not the things - you're waiting too long.

The struggle is real... it's always going to be. But it's incredibly powerful to learn to separate the two - the things and the person - and realize it's OK to still miss the things and move on. Do you miss the person or do you miss the things?

- Do you miss the companionship? Having someone to snuggle with? Always have someone around to talk with and to share your feelings with?

- Do you miss the sex? Do you miss having someone who understood what you liked and needed?

It's ok to miss those things and still move on.

- Do you miss the attraction? Do you miss the sense of confidence you had knowing that someone thought you were a big ol' bowl of oatmeal, that you were beautiful, and that you were more than enough? Physically? Personality? Everything?

It's ok to miss that and still move on.

- Do you miss someone who not only knew you so closely physically, but also knew everything about you? Someone with whom you shared everything? With whom you had no secrets?

It's OK to miss those things and still move on.

At a certain point - as tough as it might be to imagine - the association of those things with that person will fade. You don't have to hold on anymore. Healing isn't a binary experience. 0 or 1. You're always going to miss something - the attraction, the habits, the snuggles, etc.

You're always going to look back and think of how you felt. But you can move on in the midst of those feelings.

You miss having someone? You miss having a partner who is attracted to you, who helps you, who grows you, with whom you can share everything? You're human! Why wouldn't you miss those things?! It's OK to miss those things! Who wouldn't miss being supported? Who wouldn't miss having a companion? Who wouldn't miss great sex, great conversation, and having someone to grow with?

You're still human and yes... you still want those things and yes... you still miss them - BUT at a certain point, they're no longer tied exclusively to that person.

You can find them again! You can find better versions, longer lasting versions, maybe even forever versions. Just because you still miss those things… it doesn't mean you aren't free to move on.

It might not be the easiest thing you'll do, but when you can honestly say you miss the things more than the person or at minimum, you realize those things are no longer tied exclusively to the person… you're moving on.

Take a deep breath and realize that it's OK to move on in the midst of those things...

What do you miss about your last relationship?

What are three things you're most excited to find in your future partner? Be specific.

CHAPTER FIFTEEN

Tell yourself a new story

Now that we've forgiven ourselves, we've affirmed what is possible, we've celebrated the lessons, and we've practiced gratitude... it's time to tell the universe a new story.

We talked about the story you tell yourself about you and your ex in Chapter 7. Now let's zoom out... let's talk about what you believe is possible. Let's talk about your story of hope. Let's talk about your story of what you deserve.

Have you created stories in your head that look something like this?

All men want is sex. Everyone cheats. No one understands or appreciates me. No one can handle me! No one wants anything serious. No one is honest or has follow through.

Are those the types of stories you're telling yourself? It's time to get real and take responsibility for those stories. It's time to step into your worth by setting new boundaries for yourself. It's time to claim everything you've unearthed in the past 14 chapters.

The stories you tell yourself are the ones you'll end up living. Call that a cheesy thing to say or label me an overly sensitive dude, but I fundamentally believe the stories you tell yourself give the universe a sign to dish you up heaps more of the same OR to give you something different.

You're telling the universe what you want to order so why are you surprised when it serves you up a nice plate of bullsh*t? Because that's what you're ordering! I'm not surprised if that happens when you're constantly telling the universe stories of what you DON'T deserve.

Here's the truth: THOSE stories are not reflective of your worth.

You know you deserve more than those things, right? So why are you telling yourself THOSE stories? Those stories are telling the universe what to bring your way!

- If you keep telling yourself that everyone cheats, you'll keep finding people who cheat.

- If you keep telling yourself that you're only going to get hurt, you'll find someone who will hurt you.

- If you keep telling yourself that everyone disappoints you, you'll find someone who will do just that.

You can tell yourself literally any story you want. You can observe, learn, and recognize that yes, some people suck. Yes, some men are pigs and some women are crazy. Some people are dishonest and some will f**k you over. I'm not disputing that and I'm sorry you've been through that. But those stories have NOTHING to do with YOUR worth.

Know your worth by creating a strong boundary that says you do not tolerate those things or those people.

Tell yourself that! Tell yourself about your worth instead of those stories. Take responsibility for what you tell yourself.

- Do you tolerate f***boys? No! Then stop saying that all men are f***boys!

- Do you tolerate dishonesty? No! Then stop saying everyone is dishonest!

- Do you tolerate playing games? No! Then stop saying everyone is playing games!

Tell yourself a different story and watch the universe serve THAT up. Instead of crippling yourself by saying that what has happened in your dating life is the story of your life and it's all you'll ever get… flip the script and tell stories about your worth and what you actually deserve.

Tell a story that says:

There are good people out there. There are people who communicate, are driven, honest, and ready to commit and build together. There are kind, compassionate, and driven people who want what's best for me.

Tell yourself THAT story! Yes! When you take responsibility for the stories you tell yourself, you point yourself in the direction of people who respect your worth.

The universe is listening! It's more in tune with you and the stories you tell yourself than you think.

Honor yourself by creating a new boundary and change the stories you tell yourself!

Tell the universe what you want instead of what you don't.

Tell the universe what you deserve instead of what disappoints you.

Tell the universe about the boundaries you've set instead of the ways people have broken them in the past. When you do that, the universe is listening and will serve you up more of what you deserve.

Take a deep breath and tell the universe a new, more redeeming story...

What is the new story you're going to tell yourself about your dating life - past, present, and future?

CHAPTER SIXTEEN

What do YOU deserve?

Your closure is solidified by having an unwavering sense of self-worth, so let's focus on that. What do you deserve and how do you never forget it?

You deserve to feel the same love you give, the same respect you give, the same attention you give, and the same support you give.

If you're willing to give it… then without a doubt, no overthinking, no imposter syndrome… you deserve the same in return. That is it.

We're very quick to talk ourselves out of what we deserve in life because of what happened in our past. We're very quick to throw our standards out the window, lower the bar, and settle.

Sometimes that's referred to as imposter syndrome. That's the idea that we don't belong, that we're faking it and that we don't deserve success, good things, or happiness.

You can put any label on it, but it's that sinking, ever-present feeling of self-doubt. You say you deserve good things in life - success, happiness, connection with someone else, fulfillment, to be respected and loved, etc. But then you have this lingering doubt that says… but do I really? My ex proved otherwise...

You find a way to reframe your worth in life... for the worse. You find a way to justify thinking you don't actually deserve the things you say you deserve. And if you're not careful, you start to accept the bare minimum from others. Your standards take a nosedive. Your boundaries are thrown out the window.

All that happens because for some reason you've convinced yourself that you don't actually deserve the things you once thought you deserve.

But here's a quick reminder you can practice that will reset your worth. It's a simple acknowledgement...

- If you're willing to love someone, you deserve to be loved.

- If you're willing to support someone, you deserve to be supported.

- If you're willing to respect someone, you deserve to be respected.

- If you're willing to be honest with someone, you deserve to receive the same honesty.

- If you're willing to give someone time, attention, and compassion... you deserve to also receive someone's time, attention, and compassion.

Those are things I know you know you deserve! But in the heat of the moment and after a breakup... you're quick to forget this! You're pressured to forget it. Maybe even bullied into forgetting.

But this quick question grounds you and resets you back to a place where you know what you deserve.

What are you willing to do? Those are the things you deserve in return. You deserve those things! As long as you're willing to do those things you say you deserve... I don't see how it's possible you don't deserve to experience them yourself.

Sometimes it isn't returned to, yes. That's life for ya. How many times have you been hurt? How many times have you given but not received? How many times have you been compassionate and supportive but didn't receive the same? Probably quite a few.

But that doesn't mean you weren't worthy. It doesn't mean you aren't worthy. There's nothing in that equation about YOUR worth.

You deserve all the things you say you deserve. You deserve to experience the same things you're willing to give others. You deserve them for the simple reason you're willing to do them yourself. End of story.

Take a deep breath and embrace what you deserve...

What are 5 things YOU are willing to do in your dating life to get it right next time?

1.

2.

3.

4.

5.

CHAPTER SEVENTEEN

Don't give up

You bought this journal because you're someone who genuinely wants to find connection. You're willing to love, willing to try, willing to be vulnerable, and willing to be patient. BUT sometimes the universe doesn't get that memo and it serves you up a not so delicious cycle of disappointment, frustration, hurt, and betrayal.

Almost relationships. Situationships. Ghosted after 2 months. Unfulfilling and short-lived relationships. Bad first date after bad first date. Or maybe just one BIG relationship disappointment.

And so, you're about to throw in the towel. You're starting to think maybe you're unlovable. Know this...

Failed love does NOT mean you're unlovable.

Not in the slightest.

You're NOT unlovable because of someone else's inability to love you and you're not unlovable because a relationship fizzled out.

Isn't that all "failed" love is? "Failed love" is either a reflection of someone's (yours or theirs) inability to commit, inability to balance work and a relationship, inability to fight temptation, inability to be honest, etc. OR it's a reflection of lack of compatibility together.

Either way... how could that mean YOU'RE unlovable? Sure, maybe you'd do things a bit different if you could go back... but that doesn't change your worth or your lovability for the future.

When a relationship ends... your worth INCREASES. When a relationship doesn't reach its potential... your worth increases.

Think about what trial and error gets you in life. It gets you MORE. Isn't that the definition of trial and error - to try and fail with the intention of finding a permanent "winning" solution?

That's what dating is about (in a much more emotional and vulnerable manner).

So... how can your willingness to try and fail do anything but increase your worth?

It's like the gym... Sometimes the best workouts are the ones where you purposefully try to fail. You purposefully work out until you can't do another rep and you literally fail on the last one. THAT is how you build strength - so you can come back stronger.

A failed relationship has to be looked at in the same way. It's a process of intentional and vulnerable trial and error. Failed love is NOT wasted love. Failed love builds your worth.

When things don't work out with ONE person... all that means is it didn't work out with ONE person. It DOESN'T mean it won't work out with the next person and it doesn't mean you're unlovable.

When you realize that... life simply becomes about your willingness to be patient while looking and the time between failed love and final love is simply time when your worth increases.

Even if you're stuck in a pattern of failed love, it's only a pattern until it's no longer a pattern. And how do you break out of a pattern of failed love? You double down. You love more. You open yourself up to more possibilities.

Amongst the list of things you want in life... wouldn't you say finding a life-long partner is near the top? You can't expect that to come easy, right? If it's going to last a lifetime and change your life... it can't be as easy as one try, two try, LOVE.

It's going to require "failed" love. When that's your understanding of life and love, you quickly realize that failed love does NOT erode your worth. It increases it! The people who don't know how to love you simply aren't for you. The people you don't grow with aren't for you. The people you don't connect with deeply enough aren't for you.

Each one strengthens your worth. Don't give up. Don't blame yourself.

Take a deep breath and know that you are NEVER unlovable...

Are you willing to try again? Write it down.

Complete the following three times:

My ex was not the one for me because

My ex was not the one for me because

My ex was not the one for me because

CHAPTER EIGHTEEN

You'll be ready again

I'm sure you've heard the common adage that you need to love yourself first before you can love someone else. I think it goes without saying that you'll find it much easier to love someone else if you love yourself. Right? There's no disagreeing with that.

BUT we need to check ourselves a bit. There are no rules in life, and I've learned that NO… you do not need to be a fully healed, perfectly self-loving human to connect with someone else again.

It's entirely possible to love someone before you can say the same about yourself fully. We need to give ourselves permission to try again, to love again, and to let someone else in again. We need to stop putting so much pressure on ourselves to be perfect before trying again.

A mentality of "I need to love myself first" puts undue pressure on you. It can take a long time to fully love yourself, to heal from heartbreak, and to "figure out" life. If you're expecting those things of yourself today and you're waiting until you do to try again… you're waiting too long.

You don't need to be a perfectly healed, perfectly self-loving, confident person to love someone else. AND… you don't need to be that person to receive love from someone else either.

You can date and you can love. You can explore and you can connect... while you're still healing. You can date and you can love while still growing your self-love and amidst discovering yourself.

Think about your friends.

You wouldn't say you can only love your friends and you're only worthy of their love once you're healed or once you love yourself fully, right? I don't think it's a stretch to say the same is true in dating.

It's not fair to YOU to expect that you need to become "perfect" before finding perfect love.

Making sense of the world, understanding yourself and overcoming insecurities can take a lifetime. You don't need to put a wall up until you have it all figured out.

The greatest gift you can give yourself is simply letting your guard down. Respect yourself and your time and acknowledge when you're ready or not ready… but it's important to keep pushing yourself to realize you don't need to be perfect to receive love or to give love.

You don't need to be perfect to be worthy of receiving someone else's love.

As much as I don't think you should look for a relationship to complete you… I do believe in the healing and growth power that a relationship can give you.

Sometimes that's exactly what you need to find a piece of yourself, to heal a part of you, or to level up in some way.

You can love yourself before, during, and after loving someone else.

There's no right order to these things. In the grand scheme of things, yes... if you love yourself FIRST, it makes loving someone else easier. It removes a lot of uncertainty because you're more centered in who you are and what you deserve. You're not looking for total validation in someone else. But don't put yourself on the bench for too long. Do your best to love yourself, put in the inner work, take the time you need, but always remember that a rule like "you need to love yourself before you love someone else" is not always true.

Sometimes what helps you figure it all out is stepping forward when all the advice says to step back.

Take a deep breath and realize you are worthy of another shot...

> **In what ways can you let your next partner "in?" In what ways are you willing to be vulnerable with them?**

CHAPTER NINETEEN

But this time...

I'm proud of you because you're strong. But you're strong for a reason you might not consider.

A lot of the time, we think to be strong means to endure BS in life and retain our worth despite those experiences. Yes! That definitely makes you strong.

- It takes a strong person to be rejected but still know their worth.

- It takes a strong person to fall into a bad habit, disappoint themselves, disappoint others, but then turn around and create an incredible comeback story.

- It takes a strong person to establish boundaries, standards, and worth... and never lose sight of them.

Yes! That is definitely strength. BUT that's not why I'm proud of you. I'm proud of you because you recognize that there are both beautiful and ugly pieces to your story... and yet you choose to define yourself by the beautiful pieces.

Strength is refusing to be defined by your ugly traits and ugly experiences. It's easy to choose the ugly traits...

I'm an impatient person... That's just the way I am.

I'm a jealous person… That's just the way I am.

I'm a shy person… That's just the way I am.

I'm an insecure person, I'm an unsure person, I'm an introvert, I'm a lost person.

I'm a clingy person, I'm a demanding person, I'm not easy to work with, I have no self-control.

I'm a failure, nothing is working out, I'm lost, I'm hopeless, I'm falling behind.

Real strength is being aware that yes, those might be issues you wrestle with… but you have beautiful things about you.

I'm a good friend. I'm passionate. I'm reliable. I'm loyal. I'm curious. I'm disciplined. I'm compassionate. I'm empathetic.

It's not easy to be strong. It's not easy to endure the things that made you the way you are. It's not easy to face the ugly things about you, BUT to not let them define you. It's not easy to choose the one or two beautiful things about you… and let them define you. That's not easy!

It takes a strong person to realize that not only is the world NOT out to get you… but you're also NOT out to get yourself either.

That starts by choosing the beautiful things about who you are and your story and defining yourself by them instead of the ugly ones.

It takes a strong person to be at a time in his/her life where the bad outweighs the good, the rejection outweighs the success, the BS relationships outweigh the good ones... but to define yourself by the good. THAT is what makes you strong.

I'd encourage you to consider what those beautiful things might be about yourself.

I am resilient. I am reliable. I am empathetic. I am passionate.

Define yourself by those things. Those are the beautiful pieces amidst the ugly parts of your story.

Take a deep breath and embrace the closure you've created for yourself...

What are the beautiful pieces of your story?
Write as many positive affirmations about who YOU are as you can *(I am resilient. I am reliable. I am empathetic. I am passionate, etc.)*

NOW WHAT?

How do you feel right now?

Do you feel a bit lighter?

Don't feel pressure to have complete closure right now. Don't feel pressure to have it all figured out. Be proud of yourself for sitting down and being intentional with yourself. Be proud of yourself for not "waiting" for closure to be given to you. Be proud of yourself for trying.

The fact that you sat down and went inward for hours is a testament to the control you have in your life.

You are in control of the truth you live, the energy you give, and the intention you act on. Now... it's time to use the closure you've given yourself to start over.

Starting over = hitting reset and looking for what you deserve in another place, another person, another habit, or another circumstance.

We tend to think of starting over as a reflection of failure. We tend to see it as a reflection of messing up so badly that you need to start over from zero. We need to reframe what it means to start over. Starting over isn't about what you're leaving behind, it's about what you're bringing with you.

Read that again.

Think of everything you're bringing with you - the higher standards, the lessons learned, the self-worth...

When you start over, you're NOT starting from zero... you're starting over from experience. You just spent the past 2 hours remembering those experiences and what they taught you. That is powerful. You are powerful.

Moving forward, you're building on top of what you've already created for yourself because you're always bringing that power with you.

You're always starting from experience. No bad ending can take that from you. No situationship, rejection, or breakup can take that from you.

Starting over is simply the next step. It's time for your most rewarding chapter yet.

Made in the USA
Las Vegas, NV
31 August 2023